***

***

BEHIND LIES THE SUGAR

new & selectively shuffled poems

by Danny Kerwick

Cover painting by Pat Kaschalk, titled "The Woman Who Sent Her Baby To Heaven"

Back cover photo by Edgar Sierra

Published by Portals Press, New Orleans
www.portalspress.com

ISBN 978-0-9970666-0-9

© 2016 by Daniel Kerwick

Contents

Behind Lies the Sugar   9

Travelogue   41

& All That Jazz   59

4 a.m.   83

Afterword   125
  & Acknowledgments

***

around
  been around
    thanks fer askin'

content unpacked
    a lot to decipher

things to be left intact
    others scattered

up and down the block
    to the river

Raven & Jackal
    Tasmanian Tiger

    Carrier Pigeon

Girl with the Curly Hair
    articulation to self

    not about self
footprint destination

shelves of earth looking
    sideways

an itch

a tick
   yea around

   been around

thanks fer askin'

Behind Lies The Sugar

***

early one morning

the river overflowed

then

disappeared

***

1

...and here again
                              this world

yearning for sound in motionless air

the will broken   then realigned

maybe none of this was meant to stand

all unspoken

season survived to live another

                              someone says

wears a hard mask

creates little universes

                  with vast skies

        a fire   coffee from a satchel

    words suspended

                    floating on parched earth

a stolen mattress walks thru the archway

            follows an armchair

shadows like teeth against the wall

he sits in the corner

    I have my molecules in order

        he says

it's in the doing

shards of wood stack-up lovesick

succumbs to a flame

    to a tobacco pipe

the land has no water to walk on

far cry from past torrent

blood spread delta style

the wind today is sticky fingers

a painting of a japanese mountain

    hangs in the outhouse

do they have eyes these mountains

their fingers clarity of desire

    a train arriving

        an embrace

the sun burns a hole in the sky

the old dog digs another

                        lays in it

his ears swat nats and he dreams

someone is washing his feet

prepares him for the pyre

        did you find roots in the burrows

        where the river used to be

                are there enough for everyone

2

walk along the trace of where it's been

blind jagged arrow

    muddy water made us human

    separate from the giant

the power of places we pray

for departed souls

                the sky a temple

    above on a knoll

the ashes from gatherings at night

cinders in the distance from others

                we see what hovers

emerging light

        dissolving darkness

I trip and bloody my left knee

a drip to the earth

                like a red pokerchip

the old dog follows to the place

we buried his mother years ago

                          she is the dream

3

serpentine echoes reverberate

in mind's eye

steppingstones across a river

of minutes hours days decades centuries

memory working out

now's version of then

water in exile
                a ghost

crest of which
                now silence

rags we wear

shifting wind of our own

moving toward first light

vivid presence walking

the vanished esplanade

confluence of saints and devils

capturing the very form of fire itself

the lines on the palm

of your hand

tilt east   then south

then west

mudstone and sandstone

   fall

        under the gaze

   of the sun

4

tin cans on dead branch

paint images with clay

sunbeam bread girl

wrapped around flagpole

        the wonder of it

threads   floating world

the value of a wire brush

crushed seed of mustard

a rabbit   a squirrel

a sharpening stone
                unmoored

not going anywhere

a boat sits in its sediment

we enslave the vowels

guttural counterpoint pulls

across the escarpment

            remember

to mark the late day sun

5

you think of the word desire

stand alongside it

a haphazard study

seek essential nothing

           despite memories

a friend says

he has no lexicon that contains

the word for his current predicament

another hiccups in the mirror

we save pages stuck to other pages

a tangled reflection follows

clear the sorrow swarming

toward the water in the rusted cistern

           unextinguished we

this texture to feel the days with

think anecdotes of future

when people speak everyone listens

remember barely listening

muttering yea know what you mean

concerns not your concern

now inventing this

                        words attached to air

the past hangs like clouds

on the horizon

              then

                        vanish in the sky

6

roaming thru our ears

waters wrath

its baffling disappearance

                        when does it begin

Gina says we should pick the ripest

harbingers of light

find new forms of eden

Herbie twists his tongue around

charcoal faces howling

injustice   the bottle

Jonathan keeps word-treasure

close to his nose

till his turn in the fire light

to say a name a new texture

this continuum predicament

etched clarity

midnights tired fingers

say a prayer over flatbread

stars glistening shawl

pull us to tomorrows steely light

not a prayer not a plea anymore

                                        we are we

landscape beneath landscape

cling to griefs proof of love

to gather inner necessity

processional to the sunset-chair

into the night

black night falling

huddle close sweet love

quell the anger

drink bitter ale

                sing a jumbled song

      children stick together in clusters

      wary of our wariness

                      enchainment

      dream voices accumulate

              move the moondial

      where to go

                      some do

      life they dream on a mountaintop

      come back to tell us nothings there

      return with new words

                to hold onto

7

Look						The Moon

			the magician says

the river in its reflection

See

			we never left

Sweet Colleens of the Crypt of the Incurables

Sweet nowhere is here
                              Returning

    Suspended of age & pocketwatch

    O self bootstraps I am
                            Spots on hands

    Pen pokes hole in notebooks

    up trail by Tumbling Waters

    a bemusement carousel of Finger Lakes

    spread geological magic

    panting massive heart of presence

    came upon St Marys Cemetery on downslope

    generations of families

    Callahans & Coogans in the weeds

    McMahons & Mulligans   Sullivans & on & on

    lorded over by burnetts & rothschilds

    whose ivy-covered mausoleum

    supposed centerpiece as they thought

    wealth & mansion on the hill were…

In a corner of the glen

A tarnished virgin mary with broken nose

old rosarys draped on torso

Sweet Colleens in the Crypt of the Incurables

seemingly formless

                        but not powerless

crypt can't hold their lobotomy laughter

at the bloodletters

                        in wind they can dance

hover over Seneca Lake

tributaries of Allegany plateau

fish fry in Watkins Glen where Polish neighbors

whisper and cajole in VFW hall

one former german soldier sits in the corner

now hates the thought of hitler

but what did you know at 15

rifle thrust into his hands

sweet colleens polka & blow breeze

on the back of his neck

someone places fried haddock & glass of pilsner

on the table

you are here now among friends

they don't have to say

past is past   and you escaped

with the rest of us

the dead still linger of course

St Marys cemetery and all the rest

in living memory

*

In Ithaca

    white beards congregate

        on the Commons

roll their own with yellow teeth

mutter talk of impending smoking ban

    20 feet from doorways

    No park bench no mo'

court appearances for acting naturally

judge say how you do today…

Sweet Colleens in cannibus breeze

say fly with us

    coast to coast contrails

Cedar bar to Vesuvios

Rhine House in between

can Cayugas waters baptize

take the what ifs

the in-the-bushes sleepers

and redeem them

$70 fine for a cigarette

Iroqouis dream of clean water

Can gasoline turn to poetry

hills teeming with with wine tastings

acoustic music blabberings

busloads of drunken canadiens

Sweet Colleens

eyes gleeming in clouds

ever present incurable buzz

what road winding

rock and roll on

Walking in a Fugue State

                (new orleans summer)

Corner so far away

                Sycamore & Panola

Panola & Short street

                Cambronne & Green

                (wait a sec   wrong way)

    Dublin & Willow

                (street sign hanging)

                    streetcar barn say hello

Oak street hazy two block distance

drop of sweat

                drops off nose

shirt soaked with city

                (ah finally a cool breeze)

thank gods for storm comin on legs of lightning

wall of water down by southport hall

trampling pidgeontown tin roofs

sudden crash of raindrops keep fallin on my head

        duck into vietnamese corner store that

sells mostly beer   weathered old black men as if

to say weathered life twinkle eye soulful sad hangout

    hey pops   hey chief   hey white boy

buy an old english 800 24 ounce

        wait for rainbow over westbank

rain gone like it was never there

jaw with spike pete carlotta   smoke roach

scratch head of three legged dog   move to shade

listen to meandering story in the meandering

        fall into maple leaf bar

tell same story with juicy embellishments

purchase beverage from lovely Regan

sit on stool
        look in mirror peopled

            with neighborhood

*

life reshapes forward & past

to walk this pit of beatitudes

playing catch with nature

        a birth

        a nest

        a hatchling

hello daydream world

crying for more already

din of band practice

coming from dirt-floor

new orleans basement

where else would you live

follows down Plum street

              play on soldier

recirculate those ghost notes

for the season lurking

              look at her

    mother

            sitting with a book

          towers rise from earth

         look at them

               mortgaged

      leaning to the right

       bathe in tempo

            walk to muddy creek

           tadpoles and sludge

people carry noise in motion

bouncing off brick wall

anxieties and sudden yelps of joy

                        cadence of life in place

tension in body leans left
                        seeks solace

familiar seat by window

friend who is a friend

person waiting in line looks like person from past

         cheekbones   stance of torso

surrenders you back to another city

walk in reverie those streets

                        hear the voice

implicating sense of time   complicit

as world spins   slow down

lose interest in things

brain processing nothingness

                        no opinions

                bird sails past window

                    *

like clouds innocent of time

                          measure

floating canvas

                              a face says hello

        remember that day

                        laughs absurd ramblings

be well and you too

                    language a walk down the block

fold and unfold

                    concerted concert on the lawn

hammock thoughts what it means

                      music & popcorn

        educator is man and blade of grass

traditional notes
                    bended for emphasis

on far side of language

silence   symbols

part

of

what

happens

here

shimmer in veins

whisper on skin

light turns

sound of bicycle on gravel

rearrange

breath

*

    growing smaller

               before bending out of sight

  shows its length

     windows open to the breeze-heat

     O well missed the streetcar once again

        Booker and Fess

        talk with each step

        where our soul comes from

        Oak street to Dublin

        Dublin to leaky River Road

              up on levee

          the world 360

          rooftops

          and water flowing down yer back

Travelogue

life needs something

                        to be discovered

homeless guys

at Charlotte Beach Park   (7am)

                                     (Rochester NY)

scavenge cans   (5 cents each)

competition is fierce

                never seen 'em move so fast

trash barrel to trash barrel

a posse can get enough

for a 12 pack of high-octane at 8 am

when they and everyone else are legal consumers

walk regal back to beach from Circle K

                                 shopping cart parade

claim isolated picnic table not to be bothered

                                   'cept by each other

stage set

purple brushstroke backlighting

clouds hovering

like islands low on skyline of Lake Ontario

lone fisherman a speck in pier casting

rocks on batture smoothed over like sculptures

in Toronto gallery

spotlight sun clips clouds

obliterates purple-gray

shimmer follows puttering sailboat

makes way out mouth of Genesee River

enters vastness of Ontario deep

a shout from Mad Dog the chieftain

of the picnic table tribe

        Fuckin' Lynard Skynard'

        or did he say
                " I am a Lizard'

I meander past them

all my sins in a satchel

Gentle Sam waves…so does Drunkin' Jeannie

I put my toes in the sand

hundreds of gulls congregate flanked

to the west

I fill my lungs

        Brethren

                What a glorious day

        *

Gathering heart

        collecting struggle

the canvas is vast

                      (Eastern Nebraska)
low shot of grass-wind

            rises to cloud-sky

she stands in profile

            tear in her eye

carries curbed desire in vest pocket

            life becomes spiral

draws breath arms like creek branch

            off Platte River

endless   growth   wandering

            inroads & city streets

steppingstones in memory bones

stitch of land

            where they once stood

in profile

            nose to nose

        eyes and lips

  the camera pans

          inward

          gathering heart

  releases struggle

           sifts thru remains

here in the western plains

         *

What About Here
                That contains us

(no answers)   only prayers
                      (New Orleans)

slight breeze & an introduction

stand on sidewalk   hear a voice

                'assimilate don't dictate'

birdsong   yakking crows

hummingbirds busy nesting

cardinals back in town majestic

                on fencepost

horizon above rooftops

                clouds like moving mountains

denizens lumber around

                panoramic bliss

fatman down street

                smokes reefer to ease pain

people sleep dreaming rhythm

                (bass drum)

    or sit with their thoughts

                ooh poo pa do

                      (another day)

    they call us all the most

                    (heart thumps)

    The 'I' glides thru

          identity with place

    people you accompany

    nicknames

          porch

              chatter

infinity

      across stars

            & bells ringing

    see in front of me

        blocks of words   images

      speak little window frames

  unravel pebble waves on lagoon

  a child pours milk into yer shoe

        adds avocado

              bayou st john dirt

see in sky clouds alive

different tribes of geese migrating

patterns of sanskrit   squid ink

endless water of sky

on this physical plane

                        we disappear
breath
            dance
                    rhythm

brain realizes peacock

                        buddha of hello

see loose connection

of airline highway auto repair

& westbank rain

tchoupitoulas petstore

                        & uptown ladys garden

passage to noontime nap

                    clock stops

half-memory dreams her eyes

             I need no more discovery

    In backyard egret
                    gets the gecko

        in Holt Cemetary

                    get lost among spirits

        search for Jesse Hills grave

        trip on homemade tombstones

        create a disturbance in yer mind

                    (sit on bench)

                    serenity breeze flows in

        thrill distinct & visceral

        cadence holding hands

                    brief crack of light

        the musician knows

        old woman with old dog holding her up knows

        eyes backward & forward

                            time eviscerates

        this is the place

                    *

Clenched fist

        pounds shoulders

                        (Cleveland, Ohio)

on Lake Erie

                and serenity

search bridges

        between working class

        and Rockafellas

steel mill guy in Clark Bar on Clark street

wears bruise above left eye

        'thought the bastard was my friend'

takes another swig

        'hell what dont kill ya make ya fiercer

and the river is on fire

serpentine Cayahoga lit up like the 5th of july

what we wrought a memory

down in flats abandoned factorys

art gallerys & coffee emporiums

Hart Crane Memorial Sculpture Garden

Rock and Roll Hall Of Fame

    does anybody remember the James Gang

   fishfry at the Slavic hall next to the cemetery

      Widowski now a window

       Burik   Makkos   Deluca

     Levandowski now a widower

     and at dusk   beer in hand

still feel

       the hot molten steel

           *

In his variousness

leaving shadows

throughout the crowded room

                (Portland, OR)

he intimately knows

   the backdoor

the hole in the fence

   I watch him smile at the bartender

shes seen him before

riding his bike down burnside

bouncing around in front of a band

tide pull of familiarity

she to him an angel

a truancy he would love to commit

her tattooed husband in the room

he spots me by the pooltable

and the architecture of our past

produces a roll of the eyes

I point to my depleted pint

he flips me the bird

feigns empty wallet

          and buys me a drink anyway

*

The hum   rises

thru brick & mortar

pillow breath rising   (New York City)

sky up there somewhere

sun punching thru

old socks   grunt

which shoes what shirt

streel onto streets

dip and pivot   prairie dreaming

in cityscape   who are you

immensity   questioning art

elbowing ideas

          our small selves

passions headed for skating rink

central park wandering strawberry fields

wear wings like gull wings

with tenacity

hear mournful trumpeter

blow over river toward

huge bulge of American vastness

throw coins in a hat

                              move onward

                *

photographic road thinking Gordon Parks

relate foreground to background

external world internal self (Amsterdam)

mother daughter blue weather

ticking clock open window

visual touchstone returns

streetcorner scent

unimpeachable ancestor rumblings

walk canals in shank of evening

                        frames worlds transparent

      fear   allure

      exile   in   footprints

                    daughters indignant stare

fisherman with a pipe

a calloused hand clasps a forearm

an artist to the subject

the subject attacks the artist

      stands up and dusts off itself

& all that jazz

MONGUS & MINK

for paul pines

on tip of tongue

and fingers gesturing

just one of those things

like missing last train

out of Hackensack after

wednesday night prayer meeting

words mangled but so what

eat that chicken and clutter

in yer muttered room Spooner

Epistrophy dysphonia always

round midnight Skippy

beneath the stuttering underdog

    an epitaph

        straight no chaser

goodbye pork pie hat

no regrets

mongus and mink   shit

ya know where I mean

THE ORCHESTRA HAS LEFT THE BUILDING

sheet music on lecturn

an empty room

the conductors in prison

remembers only Art Tatum

whistles forbidden rhythms

he danced once in his life

terrified of flaxen-haired

girls smile her hand roaming

at his spine

put melody away and forget it

future idioms after unnamed revolution

decommissioned sculpture pigeonshitted

and graffitied

underlying emotions recognized

by greek chorus wearing kilts

    singing a language yet to be determined

    while the city sleeps objectivists

    zigzag to the bank

    mumbles of streetsweepers collectively

    a treasure hidden from all of us

    a silent complacency for the obvious

                          company

        the door opening

                          the sound

        a multitude of souls

FOR TIM GREEN   aug 31st 2014

At confluence

river   mind   sound

walks down blocks of triangled neighborhood

      words   sight   fever

  how

        was

            the

                    gig

        another

         shared space

        flesh   &   voice

        anticipation of rhythm

    friend hits cymbal   bass drum

    echo room

            room echo

and there he is

                here you are

soft slow halting   long expression

life expression

ego no more than a smile

a nod   time to listen

compassion

& all that jazz

and in his passing

a blow to the real deal

fading   that notion

but all needed is a spark

flash   spark

laughing bassline

converse the keys   black & white

pearly sweat on brow

down to it

revere the dust

the light

the click of time

harbor snug   keystone corners

blue notes

    cigar on balcony on blue nile

  wand of Mississippi   spellcast

    thought of
          thought

                there

      in his hands

ANOTHER TIME IN A SILENT WAY

    song for Joe Zawinul & Samuel Beckett

another time in a silent way

learning squandering the riverrun

wandering the twisted embankment

echo's bones & herd

of bull in the eye

cucumber slumber

a drunken boat abandoned

Ben Webster in window morning

East River slogging along

Viennese immigrants bickering

time ticks along

Pacific sun

a foggy bridge to Oakland

in a silent way

the funk began

fusion damn straight

synthesized lovers & vaudevillian pathos

Buster Keaton did dance in bump city

Cannonball mercy mercy mercy

an amputee makes his way down the alley

war medals jangling

to see this never gone again

a passage repeated   inverted

birdland in backyard   musing

imagines

                a voice comes to one in the dark

timeless in a silent way

teaching sound in mind

on the street

on the page

BLUE DISTANCE

In the early dawn

steal what you see

what you read on the horizon

don't
         mention

                 symbolism

click the camera obscura

panorama in a bowl

St Augustine   Florida

has nice beaches

horrible tourists

how language uses us

in gods willyness

reach blind for a book
                any book

from the accumulation

    direction secured

               proves displacing

if determined world

               questions

               what compelled it

               no one is going anywhere

magic precarious

               that protects us

               an unreflective fact

invention discredited

               by its inventor

                     and her mask

containment rattles
               the windowpane

perceptions complex
                     itself

its potential
                     death

               in all its variousness

UNTOLD FLOATING NICKLE

sincere irony on bedpost dream

                                         eyes like spiders

arms reach for castenets

happy spinning world

voice echo forgets to close window

stars hammer

the purple blue lake

Beckett says touch both left hands

A little like October

wind blusters and she creaks

page turning down Dublin street

lost key returned

                             the terror of love

the blessing

to awake with oneself

knowing it was there

                                        never gone again

ATTACH IT TO EARTH

Muddy night

                alluvial plain of denizens

stagger down hallway out back

to smoke room picnic tables

                   under Cassiopeia

Big Dipper

           Neon Mug O Beer

attach it to earth

always   floating

whispers nailed to smoke

      there are no eyes harder to catch

than the barman who wishes he was fishing

no alternatives

as grain of wood peaks thru varnish

a woman named Sam is moving to Alaska

drinks rye whiskey with her pickled pigs feet

runes . rituals . floating eyes

move hard in the whitening light

it's time to go home but no one moves

barley sandwich for breakfast

someone asks

                why Turkish bath

                massage Swedish

Bumfuck alliteration

                say the man wearing glasses

                reinventing himself in the mirror

Nick Tahoe's never closes

garbage plate $2.99

Terminal Lounge long gone

 each moment less future to worry about

            attach it to earth

 and barman
                          get Sam another one

STORY POEM: Neighborly Fictionist

                                    for JT

it started 2 days after they moved in

a change in tone   muffled thru the sheetrock

screeches and sobs that soon turned rancid

cussing that sounded alternately like

a rottweiler and Chihuahua

in less than a week the dam broke

glasses and bottles hurled

shattering into silence

only to escalate again and again

a runaway freight train careening

down magazine street

i thought of calling the police

but refrained

one 4 AM banging on the wall

finally quelled their loving bloodthirst

and laying wide awake

first sign of light thru window

dumptruck commerce commenced

i got up

leaned in the bathroom pissing

thinking

what sweet dreams

they must be mustering

      my new neighbors

a visiting poet i admired

was reading in town

and calmed by the landscape

of his words   the edge   the glint

his openness to contradictions and

narrative navigations

i timidly approached the bespectacled writer

during the break

especially liked the ballerina piece

i said to him i've been there

what can you do with gangsters like that

whatever did happen i inquired

he looked at me   said

what do you mean

when the fire broke out

they were trapped in the bathroom

what happened after that ?

he then looked at me with pity

and laughed

it's written in the first person

but my life's not that episodic

i just like putting syllables together

95 percent pure fiction

I now knew what the book jacket

meant by the conundrum of moral aesthetic

my o my i trudged back home confused

what a terrible week

marauding neighbors

          and poets who lie!

i opened my gate

digging for my house keys

when the couple next door

exited their hovel

looking sweet as newlyweds

grinning thru their bruises

oh i say   and suddenly my voice

fatherly   like that of the poet

listen neighbors i need to talk

I know that couples fight

heat of passion and all that

but let me tell you a story

many moons ago

hill and dales away from here

i lived next to a young couple

not unlike yourselves

they would seem blessed one day

and the next day daggers

screaming at each other

at the top of their lungs

when one dark blustery night

someone couldn't take it anymore

a gun was pulled

shots were fired

and the night turned silent

my neighbors looked at me in horror

who they asked what happened

i employed a pregnant pause

and smiled

put my key in the lock and said

what do you mean

4 am

4 am

        King of the world

sleepy dreamers

                in other rooms

pin drop in studio

    objects

          in stasis

                shimmer

place for coffee cup

armature on easel

          no sound

                without magic

Time stopped

        She opens door to garden

daughters flowers   green ruffage

and rabbits

        under cherry laurel living

simple power   delivers vision

        nothing heroic

form and light

                chance disposition

self tremor   deep down

minds-eye to tip of brush

paint under coat of secret soul

4 AM

    moon   a gold coin

  tossed up

    on a blue black tarp

sound of urban rooster crow

    breaks the stillness

             and echoes

an egret perched on chimney

    sillouette in stars

waits for glint-flash on fishpond

    for early snack

sneak

        a shot of wine

think of a touch

as if you are touched

drink fingers

thru entire body

there is no floor under you

get old   get young

get old again

lose sight

to beginning murmurs

it has dimension

try to lift

what you see

ascend

without wings

fail better

someone said

horizon dies

dark turns to darkness

an aggression

timelessness

Ms Rosemary   down the street

    sits on her porch

    sews gold into clothing

        waits for church bells

            to ring
   neighbors to greet

       sketch her likeness

         tack to studio wall

adorn the borders

                    of living object

mix color with wax

                    for heavens texture

get old   get young

        get old again

remember walk on levee

          at twilight

then paint yourself

                out of the picture

    the egret flies

               over sleepy dreamers

    houses starlit yards

    as rabbit leaps for burrow

    Ms Rosemary has moved

              back to Alabama

    fingers her rosary

              and prays

        another day begins

in this place

              to be made
or found

discipline

           or haphazard

simple light

          works the sky

landscape pulls us

           together

overcomes death

            another moment

from **You Stand Alongside Desire**

you stand alongside desire

                                      The city

                The light in the wave of a hand

you stand alongside revolving mirrors

              landscape of braincage

                        searching scraps of memorabilia

ripping bits of wisdom

                        armature for day

                        cushion for night

it was October

you thought you were going to die

                    standing at the ferry terminal

      another day waiting on a train

                        sitting in a pub

            afterimage

                                    exhaling

undo the hours

        trampled stops and starts

to the moment she says

        the stars are not falling tonite

        its alright

the reply is silence

slow strange walk of contentment

        culture can't be entered

        ticket bought for   you say

our wandering led to chance

        desire is in our eyes

                she replied

first touch of hands

last ferry across the shimmer

        how could you know

        her smile shadow would follow

        *

the world

in the back of his head

                    is out of time

finds spiritual biography

in the words of others

broken rain a friend calls it

dali-typhoon another

he haunts the aisles of university libraries

seeks skinny books of poesy

waiting to be plugged in
                    charged up

cryptically initials the due date chart

                    the busted hourglass

                    axis of years dispersed

                    twinkling with history

*

wondering how the language

      of distance

                kisses midnight

i can point to it on a map

dress the town in comprehensible

            just as it is

were we swimming there

hearing thunder as a kind madness

      *

in our heavens

           the blink of an eye

                      tasting the wet electric

eyes and confessions

                  lady matisse gazes

the blacksmith shop now has neon

                      bamboo tables

smiling faces of mascot insects

       the sky darkens as the word darkens

                *

love in our gropes

the clock on the wall

beloved Chartres street teeming

gradations of youth

    were we swimming there

    hearing thunder as a kind madness

    wearing our heavens

    the end of that heaven

the man was coming with a condor smile

and we knew it

tumbling down Toulouse street

we cleared space

    racked up miles

live with a twisted pocket watch

walk with ghosts in alleyways

    *

I've seen him with no fixed

itinerary in mind

clutching his imagination

as if inside a toy chest

his presence is undercover

                                        untouchable

the past a sound

                    in the shadow mountains

                *

night bring it's flank

                         hum and glow

there are no puzzles to scatter

thought finds a place

mirror image meets the image

death touched others

who touch

                         the other

bridges to abandoned buildings

rub shoulders with faces of belief

incarnation reflects

                         things below the surface

a temple behind the eyes

*

there you are

                she replies

are you gathering heart

collecting struggle

have colors of fate

taken you to the right place

you stand alongside desire

                        the city

the light in the wave of a hand

there is no mess thing this morning

prayers were said

                a temple behind the eyes

abandon yourself

in the marrow of landscape

allow the horizon

to settle its own arguments

you stand alongside selves

invited to the garden

a turn along the avenues

                                          blue horizon

I will try to recognize you

                                          and failing

can still say hello

from **Wave out of Water**

to believe we can sneak away

                                        from old lives

be complete without them

neighborhood voices

as if not hearing them before

       them   them

are not forces

                                    against us

but part of sidewalk paths

curving round this planet

                                    conspiring within you

& that guy down the block

hat on his head

                 looks up at the clouds

and says

                                    clouds

in death of friend

a wonder of self

how parts of departed

    smile   gesture

        voice

                      that time

  remembering   dreaming

        gathering

    a wave out of water

letting self

                fall

        from cliff-dream...

Nov 2005

    1

at rise

the horizon sees as we do

half dream and shadowy hope

waiting for someone to show

the garden to the tourists

empty wasp's nest and granite bench

mind-trinkets bloody married

the bleary go to jail if they could

    one thin window

    gawk at the muse

    key just out of reach

it's seasons like this

that want for another

feet gathering splinters

is how we say good morning

the shining prize is not forthcoming

it waits in the hallway

with the dust

      2

at night

overhead wingstrokes

like desperate breath

my owls-head blinking

beer addled   what street

which window eyes

is lost temporary

or etched in crows feet

spin the globe   use penis

pack unnecessaries

hop coach to anonymity

a door opens

iridescent mist

streetlamp glow unattainable

seems imaginary

whisper not bloodbank or ghosttown

silence can fool you

flap wings

hear denizen's dreams

they speak of what we

have in common

from **L Notes**

The old man said

  she owned no coffee table

  lived cribbled under indifferent stars

  backporch Chicago

  barbeque in a blizzard

  german white thighs

  black smoke

  what prism of what eyes

  sequesters a day

  old mans last lap

  around the race track

  you have to love something a littlle

  to give it some grief

  to dismiss means you were never there

  head lost in vanities

The visitor walks into St Boniface Cemetery

as cottontail at gate hops away

names carved in granite

Zuranski Konopasek Toussaint

Immigrant in Chicagoland dream

Swallow the citywork the jungles stone walls

Sandburg's template

cats footprints steam Halstead

plucked on a rusty typewriter

using single syllabled keys

mote smoke   sear that

check what   roof gaze

carve out soiled sunlight

shellacked streets watched

by a battle colored sky

word play steel shanked

anonymous warmth
                        of heart moon

The visitor lingers

    where Nelson Algren lingered

    with sharpened scalpels and a cigar

    if alive today would he write

    The Man with the Golden Cellphone

    or sit in Humbolt Park feeding the ducks

    sheltered by magnificently lumbering museums

    exquisite corpses   cuticles of grand pianos

    Dekooning excavations of avenues faces

    shuddering poverty crouched

                in Wabash doorway

prefer no particular spire

champion no particular people

(perhaps bears

bulls blackhawks)

city split in two

(cubs or sox)

tolerate tired faces

rub shoulders

up iron staircase

to platform

the rumbling L takes you where....

And the living

Fred Anderson pockets yer 10 spot

at door of his Velvet Lounge on Indiana ave

his journey from Monroe Louisiana

blues to bop in blood up alleyway delta

to southside chinatown

where he throws charlie parker ghost notes

 at the younger players

 Von Freeman at the Apartment

 John Primer at Buddy Guys Legends

northsiders mingle at the Green Mill

after-partys at someones crib

     tell us please

Once under ice now filled

to brim level dirt occasional

alien boulders in sporadic woodland

Illinois Basin humps over Kankakee Arch

down thru Calumet to Hyde Park bookstore

where the visitor lets snippets

titles & passages

cross eye-brain

dead words live in palm of hand

Frank Lloyd Wright proclaims

        night time is the right time

                to raise the roof

Prairie grass   inland sea

Cicero to Joliet

swift to mockery

slow to love

cigar man with pockerchips

            round the table

 Polk Tuggle Herbst

 Sergio Gregorio

 Katy & Jack

 Andre Williams on 7th floor

 of Belair Hotel

 white rum in warm glass

 plans train ride south

 in spring

Investigate chance

ain't no letter you can send

mind-stroll thru parks & avenues

mark consciousness

name of neighborhood

on Argyle street spied

ghost of Carl Solomon

(what was he doing here)

pointing at his own head

trapped in doorway

tolerated by Vietnamese shopowner

with broom in hand

who understands

                        lonely madness

exile

Illusions expecting

                importance

of course

to see eyes on lake sinking

empty window chill-out

low-down shakes

Diversey Street SRO

flood come and gone

with it a cleansing

itinerant migration

to new faces

black box theatre doing Beckett

hot dog with peppers

& tomatoes

a walk to an Old Style sign

on pavement

outside thrift store

on Lincoln

little green finch

with orange eyebrows

stunned from flight

into window

          didn't kill him

three of us humans gather

not knowing what to do…

the visitor (I)

bends down touch its plume

and sudden as a heart attack

flies over honking traffic

Put yer hand on map

of North America

Gulf of Mexico to Great Lakes

middle finger Chicago

                        he's still here

bones dance deep

in Lake Michigan

remembered by barstool ghosts

who smile while

                        crying their losses

      our breath

             we fall

                      into one another

this six feet under

this levee elegant cage

words are fresh air

voices weave

                smoke and electricity

decay   always the decay

unlevel   but the walking shoes

chattering parrots in palms

prayer in our bones

silence a polished rock

busted sidewalk

              conquered by giant oak

word roots inching along

underworld rise to be spoken

nothing truly wavers

strange potent flavor in night air

treeline thoughts and doubts

   back to the core

      unarmored

invisible skeletons

in separable from skin

no destiny in meander

      but there you are

  and yes

     it is nice to see you again

AFTERWORD:

Discovered Methodology

The poem *Behind Lies The Sugar* included in this collection was first published in 2008 as a handmade limited edition by my own Simpatico Poets Press with help from the letterpress maestro Peter Anderson and a slew of others who graced the podiums of our various gatherings at bars, libraries, coffee shops, bookstores and inpromtu backyard soiree's here in New Orleans. It was DIY at its very best with numerous other small presses strutting their stuff.

As poets the thought that we stand on the shoulders of those who came before us is a given but I enjoy standing next to living poets cajoling, bantering and hopefully listening. The musical sounds that are the rhythm of language, blocks of words displaying and disputing their drumbeats, fugue notes rising up in an individuals' voices are (to me anyway) at the core of what poetry is, apart from their charming cousins prose and creative nonfiction.

I lean toward 'all poems one poem' school of thought and will use current workpages and old poems to create new verse, not as an improvement persay only as another usage within the vocabulary of my own breath. At open mic readings I tend to read workpages to see if the cadence and breath of the lines are getting somewhere, however funky. That said, I also very much enjoy spoken word, prose poems (hopefully surreal) or someone just venting their opinions (hopefully with humor). There's room for everyone but it's the music of language that opens the door with many landscapes pouring forth. Context is in the ears of the listener says the man by the river, and taking cue from jazz improvisors who intuitively cull from the symbol-sounds and associations they have played from the vast catalogue they have experienced, poets seek the hanging threads that are all around us. I shared with the young poets in my professor-friend John

Roche's class at RIT a piece of verse and related that I'd watched migrating birds as I waited for a bus, read from a book by Achebe who had written something about the ocean that is sky and as my pen hit paper some words a friend had related to me about his knowledge of squid ink and the history of the written word. Here's what I scribbled in my notebook:

>'see in sky clouds alive
>different tribes of geese migrating
>patterns of sanskrit   squid ink
>endless water of sky
>on this physical plane
>we disappear'

To make particular from various sources, in this case a visual experience, a bit of thievery from reading and intuitive rhythmmaking (sanskrit...squid ink) to create a verse that is then jigsawed into a poem that is jigsawed into a manuscript is the magic that never quite gets there. And thanks to that, if it did we'd quit writing poetry!

In this collection is also included what I call a 'Story Poem' or what I argue is a lazy short story, because it really is prose broken up into shorter lines. I'm guilty of my own petpeeve! I would especially rail against myself if it were a single piece in a journal with my name on it (Please no! I'm not that kind of poet!) But put in the context of the 'one poem' that is this book, the travelogue of words it didn't seem out of place. Also the subtext of the story is one of my (and it seems others) favorite poetics debates that is 'poet as fictionist' or 'poet as memoir diarist'. I've had fun conducting a workshop where i command 'you cannot use 'I' until the tenth line' and witnessing the twisting of brows of some of the writers who are more prone to write from personal experience than just purely a love of
language.

Borges said that 'like all abstract words the word metaphor is a metaphor' or greek for 'transfer', two terms, one of which briefly transformed into another. Hopefully logic lurks underneath and thats where a hint of narrative prose, or lines anchored in a sense of place help the train down the track with many surprises along the way. You may think that you're writing about the mountain but end up throwing out the mountain.

The reason for subtitling this book *New & Selectively Shuffled Poems* is that along with new pieces, some of the older lines are put in new contexts. Language is transient, morphs itself with the crows and crashing waves. New forms away from my own consensus. Intellect can get in the way and putting yourself beyond language, tiptoeing thru an intuitive landscape and hopefully bemusing yourself and others can be a satisfying journey for a poet. It has been for me.

Enjoy the book and feel free to steal some phraseology.

Danny Kerwick
New Orleans Nov 2015

Acknowledgments

Some of the verse in this book first appeared in *The Cafe Review*, *The Maple Leaf Rag*, *Yawp*, *Subhouse*, *Foothills*, *Big Bridge* and other publications. A few poems were included in Lisa D'Amour's play *Airline Highway* which has had productions in Chicago and New York.

Thanks to the long-running Maple Leaf Bar Reading Series and its indefatigable host Nancy Harris & and all the regular misfits (you know who you are); to the Dragon Den and The Gold Mine Saloon; to Dave Brinks, Jimmy Ross, Megan Burns, JP Travis, Bill Lavender, Joseph Makkos, Gina Ferrara, Jonathan Kline, Thaddeus Conti, Carolyn & Michael Czarnecki of Foothills Publishing, Pat Kaschalk & Poppy Miles, Lewis Schmidt, John Roche, Tim Polk, Rick Petrie, Norm Davis, Lisa D'Amour, Brendan Connelly, Jethro the Catahoula, the Mexican squealers of Audubon Park, and a special shoutout to my poet friend & mentor Paul Pines for his still-going-strong-fortitude and inspiration.

www.ingramcontent.com/pod-product-compliance
Lightning Source LLC
Chambersburg PA
CBHW020940090426
42736CB00010B/1208